Original title:
New Beginnings

Copyright © 2024 Swan Charm
All rights reserved.

Author: Mirell Mesipuu
ISBN HARDBACK: 978-9916-79-200-1
ISBN PAPERBACK: 978-9916-79-201-8
ISBN EBOOK: 978-9916-79-202-5

The Pilgrimage to Truth

In silence we tread upon sacred ground,
With hearts wide open, truth shall be found.
Each step a prayer, a whisper of grace,
Guided by light, we seek His embrace.

Through valleys of doubt and shadows of fear,
We journey together, our purpose is clear.
In every struggle, His presence abides,
A beacon of hope, where love truly resides.

Mountains may rise, but our spirits will soar,
With faith as our compass, we long for much more.
The path may be winding, the road overgrown,
Yet each breath we take brings us closer to home.

In fellowship's bond, we share in the song,
With voices united, we know we belong.
Through trials and triumphs, our souls intertwine,
A tapestry woven, a design so divine.

As we reach the summit, the truth shines so bright,
Illuminating hearts, dispelling the night.
We gather as one, our pilgrimage ends,
In the arms of the Father, where love never bends.

Serenity in the Shift

In whispered prayers, the dawn breaks bright,
Guiding our hearts to the sacred light.
Through shifting sands, we find our way,
In faith we stand, come what may.

The heavens tremble with love's decree,
A symphony sung for you and me.
In trials faced, our spirits soar,
Embracing peace forevermore.

Like rivers flow, so do we bend,
Trusting the path our souls have penned.
With open arms, let worries cease,
In the shift, we find our peace.

Destined to Rise

From ashes cold, our hopes ignite,
In darkness deep, we seek the light.
With hearts aflame, we rise anew,
Destined to shine, this much is true.

In valleys low, our spirits fight,
With faith as wings, we take our flight.
Together, bound by love's embrace,
We journey forth, through time and space.

The stars above, they call our name,
With every step, we're not the same.
In unity, we find our eyes,
Awake again, we're destined to rise.

In the Arms of Renewal

In gentle hands, our burdens cease,
As hope descends, we find our peace.
In sacred moments, we are free,
Cradled softly, eternally.

With breath anew, we face the dawn,
In love's embrace, all fears are gone.
Through every trial, we will grow,
In the arms of renewal, our spirits glow.

Each tear that's shed, a prayer of grace,
Guiding us to our rightful place.
With open hearts, we rise above,
In the arms of renewal, we find love.

The Offering of Today

In every moment, a gift bestowed,
The offering of today, our humble road.
With gratitude, we seek the way,
Embracing all that comes to stay.

In laughter shared, and tears released,
We gather strength, our souls appeased.
With open arms, the world we greet,
The offering of today, so sweet.

In kindness deep, we plant a seed,
For love and hope are all we need.
With every heartbeat, the promise stays,
Within the offering of these days.

Baptism of the Soul

In waters deep, purification flows,
The heart, once heavy, now freely glows.
With whispers soft, the Spirit calls,
As grace descends, and in love we fall.

In sacred moments, the past is washed,
A promise made, a burden tossed.
With every drop, a new life springs,
In unity, we rise on faith's wings.

Heaven's Gentle Touch

Beneath the stars, a peace unfolds,
In quiet night, a warmth that holds.
The whispers of angels, soft and clear,
Guiding our hearts, dispelling fear.

With every breath, a sacred song,
In heaven's light, we all belong.
A gentle touch, divine embrace,
In love we find our rightful place.

Awash in the Spirit's Joy

A river flows with joyous sound,
In every heart, a love unbound.
Awash in grace, our spirits dance,
In laughter bright, we take our chance.

The sun arises, glowing bright,
With each new dawn, we find delight.
The spirit sings, a vibrant choir,
In joy we rise, forever higher.

The Tapestry of Renewal

Threads of life, both dark and bright,
We weave together in sacred light.
With every knot, a story spun,
In tapestry rich, we all are one.

The hands of time, they gently guide,
Through valleys low, and mountains wide.
In renewal's dance, we find our way,
Embracing grace, day by day.

Fragrance of the New Dawn

In morning light, the world awakes,
With whispers soft, the spirit breaks.
Each petal blooms, a prayer raised,
In nature's song, we stand amazed.

The sun's warm glow, a sacred sign,
In every heartbeat, love divine.
As shadows flee, hope's breath is near,
In gentle grace, we cast off fear.

Cleansing Waters of Grace

Beneath the skies, the rivers flow,
In crystal waves, the mercies sow.
With every drop, a sin erased,
In liquid light, our souls embraced.

As pools reflect the heavens' glow,
We find our path where waters go.
In quiet depth, our burdens leave,
Through cleansing streams, we learn to believe.

Songs from the Horizon

The dawn unfolds with melodies,
In every note, the spirit breathes.
Songs carried forth on faith's sweet air,
In harmony, we find our prayer.

With open hearts, we dare to sing,
Proclaiming light, new life to bring.
In every chord, a promise made,
For in this song, our hope won't fade.

Unchained by Love's Embrace

In tender grace, we find our home,
No longer lost, no need to roam.
Each binding chain, in Love's sweet light,
Is cast away, renewed in sight.

With arms stretched wide, we face the day,
United strong, our fears at bay.
In Love's embrace, we rise above,
Transformed anew, we live and love.

Under the Veil of Grace

In quiet whispers, hope does weave,
A tapestry of love to receive.
Beneath the veil of wisdom's grace,
We find our hearts in sacred space.

In trials faced, we learn to see,
The strength bestowed, eternally.
Through shadows cast, He lights our way,
Guiding spirits, come what may.

With open hearts, we bend our knee,
In gratitude, our souls agree.
The journey's end, a promise sweet,
In every step, His love complete.

A grace that flows, like rivers wide,
In every soul, our hearts collide.
Together in faith, we rise and sing,
The joy of life, our offering.

Transcending pain, the spirit soars,
Through grace we seek, and find the doors.
With every breath, we trust the call,
Together in love, we conquer all.

Dare to Dream Anew

In the stillness of the night,
Stars awaken, filled with light.
Hope ignites a gentle flame,
Dare to dream, in His name.

Beyond the doubts, beyond the fear,
Voices whisper, clear and near.
With faith as anchor, hearts will soar,
Dare to open every door.

The past may linger, shadows cast,
But new horizons shine at last.
In every heartbeat, visions grow,
Dare to step where few will go.

Together we rise, hand in hand,
Build the future, understand.
With every dream, God's promise blooms,
In every heart, a world that looms.

So dare to dream, embrace the sky,
With wings of faith, we learn to fly.
For in each dream, a truth bled through,
God's love awaits, in all we do.

Wonders of a Shining Path

Upon the road where blessings flow,
A shining path, where spirits glow.
In every step, a light appears,
As love unfolds, it calms our fears.

Through valleys low and mountains high,
His gentle hand will lift us nigh.
With every struggle, heart embraced,
Wonders bloom in sacred space.

In unity, we find our song,
A chorus sweet, where we belong.
With open hearts, we seek the way,
In gratitude, we humbly stay.

The journey paved with grace and truth,
A testament to endless youth.
In every moment, blessings cast,
The shining path will hold us fast.

So walk in faith, embrace the light,
For every shadow yields to bright.
In wonder's grasp, we find our part,
A shining path, a joyous heart.

Journeying into Light

Across the fields of time and grace,
Our souls embark, a holy race.
With faith as compass, hearts aligned,
Journeying into light, we find.

Through trials faced and lessons learned,\nThe flame of love within us burned.
With every tear, redemption flows,
In every heart, His mercy grows.

Together we seek the sacred spark,
Illuminated, we shun the dark.
With every prayer, we rise above,
Journeying forth, wrapped in His love.

With every dawn, a promise new,
The golden rays, a guide so true.
In peace we tread, our spirits free,
Journeying on, eternally.

So take my hand, and let us roam,
In every heart, we find our home.
For in His light, our souls unite,
Journeying into love's pure light.

The Kingdom of Possibility

In the realm where dreams ignite,
Faithful hearts take flight.
Every soul a shimmering star,
Guided by a light from afar.

Hope blooms like morning dew,
In whispers soft and true.
A tapestry woven divine,
With threads of love that intertwine.

The path is paved with grace,
Each step an embrace.
In the silence of the night,
Possibilities shine bright.

Hands reach out to dare,
With a spirit laid bare.
In unity, we shall roam,
Together we find home.

For in this sacred place,
We gather, face to face.
The kingdom vast and free,
Awaits for you and me.

Echoes of Rebirth

From ashes we arise,
Under endless skies.
Each heartbeat a fresh start,
Renewed with every part.

The whispers of the past,
In memories are cast.
Yet in grace, we are shown,
That love, once sown, is grown.

Streams of mercy flow,
Cleansing every woe.
With the dawn, new light breaks,
In every soul, a change awakes.

The cycle of life unfolds,
A story yet untold.
Embrace the gift of now,
With humble hearts we vow.

In the garden of the soul,
We all are made whole.
With every breath we take,
Echoes of rebirth we make.

Wings of Divine Ascent

Lifted high on wings of grace,
We journey to that sacred place.
Each prayer a feather light,
Soaring through the endless night.

With faith our compass true,
We find strength, me and you.
Guided by an unseen hand,
Together we shall stand.

Mountains bow under love's might,
Every challenge a pure delight.
In unity, we shall rise,
With hearts open to the skies.

Heaven whispers soft and clear,
Inviting us, drawing near.
With every step, we transcend,
On wings where love won't end.

In the embrace of the Divine,
We wear His light as a sign.
Together we'll ascend,
With a hope that won't bend.

The Scroll of Redemption

Written on the heart's own scroll,
Are tales of grace that make us whole.
In every line, a chance to mend,
The story of love without end.

Through trials faced and tears shed,
A path where faith has led.
Each chapter turns with intention,
Unfolding our divine ascension.

In shadows, light finds ways,
To turn our nights into days.
With every word, we reclaim,
The sacred truth, our flame.

The scroll reveals our worth,
Each moment a rebirth.
With compassion woven deep,
In our souls, love we keep.

For every heart's desire,
Is kindled by this fire.
In the scroll, we find our song,
Together, we all belong.

Seeds of Faith Take Root

In the garden of the heart, we sow,
Whispers of grace in the soil below.
With the light of hope, each sprout will rise,
Reaching for the heavens, touching the skies.

Tended with love, through sun and through rain,
Each prayer a seed, no effort in vain.
Roots intertwine in the depths of the soul,
Together they flourish, becoming whole.

Through seasons of doubt, the flowers bloom bright,
Guided by faith, we walk towards the light.
In unity's song, our spirits entwine,
For the garden of life is sacred, divine.

Every tear shed waters what will arise,
In the rich earth of dreams, the future lies.
With steadfast hearts, we nurture and wait,
For the harvest of love to embrace our fate.

The Sacred Turn of the Wheel

In the quiet of dawn, the wheel turns slow,
A cycle of grace, where blessings flow.
From birth unto death, the dance of the day,
Eternity whispers, guiding the way.

With each turn of fate, shadows may fall,
Yet the light of the spirit will answer the call.
In every lament, a lesson of peace,
The rhythm of life, a gentle release.

The wheel spins 'round, in harmony's song,
With faith as our anchor, we know we belong.
Through trials and triumphs, we move in grace,
As the sacred wheel turns, we find our place.

In the twilight's embrace, we stand as one,
Connected in love, our journey begun.
With every rotation, hope's flame ignites,
Illuminating paths, our spirits take flight.

A Promise in the Morning

As dawn breaks the silence, a promise is made,
In the golden light, all fears will fade.
With each breath of hope, the soul is restored,
A new day unfolds, and faith is adored.

Through clouds of uncertainty, the sun will peek,
A whisper of grace for the weary and weak.
Hold on to the light that flickers within,
For every new dawn is where life can begin.

In cascading rays, find solace and strength,
A heart that is open will go to great lengths.
With love as our compass, we navigate fate,
In the promise of morning, let us celebrate.

For every lost moment will sweetly return,
In the warmth of the sun, our spirits will burn.
Embrace the new day, let hope's anthem ring,
For in every sunrise, the joy that it brings.

The Resurrection of Dreams

From ashes of doubt, our visions arise,
In the depths of the soul, where passion lies.
With wings of the spirit, we learn to ascend,
In the resurrection of dreams, we find our blend.

Each hope buried deep, is a seed that will sprout,
Nurtured by faith, it will shatter all doubt.
With each passing moment, we rise and we learn,
For the fire of longing forever will burn.

Through struggle and strife, the spirit takes flight,
Bringing forth visions that dance in the night.
The dreams of the past weave the fabric of now,
In the tapestry of life, we honor the vow.

So rise, dear heart, let your dreams take command,
With love as you guide, take a bold stand.
In the resurrection of what once seemed lost,
We find strength in the journey, no matter the cost.

A Lantern of Fresh Insight

In the dark, a light shines bright,
Guiding souls to what is right.
Wisdom flows like waters clear,
Bringing peace, dispelling fear.

Hearts ignite with sacred flame,
Each spark calls a sacred name.
In the still, a truth unfolds,
A gentle warmth that never scolds.

With each step, a new embrace,
Finding God in every space.
Through our trials, hope arises,
In our prayers, the world surprises.

Let compassion be our guide,
With faith walking by our side.
In each whisper, love we find,
A lantern bright, for all humankind.

The Symphony of Tomorrow

In the dawn, a chorus sings,
Notes of peace and hope it brings.
Every heart, a part of this,
In unity, we find our bliss.

Harmony through every trial,
Lifting spirits, mile by mile.
In the dance of time so vast,
Promises of joy unsurpassed.

Gentle rhythms guide our way,
Crafting dreams from night to day.
Let the melody be our prayer,
To the heavens, love we share.

With each heartbeat, let us stand,
Working together, hand in hand.
For the future holds a song,
A symphony where we belong.

Echoing the Spirit's Whisper

In the silence, voices call,
Echoes dancing, over all.
From the depths, the spirit speaks,
In the stillness, solace seeks.

Gentle nudges, soft and clear,
Guiding souls to draw near.
In our hearts, the truth ignites,
Illuminating sacred sights.

With each breath, a prayer we share,
Renewing faith in quiet air.
Let compassion be our quest,
Finding strength in every test.

Through the whispers, love we hear,
Uniting all, both far and near.
In the echo, joy resides,
A melody where peace abides.

The Shift of Sacred Ground

As the earth begins to shift,
Hearts entwined, we share our gift.
In the struggle, grace appears,
Transforming pain, drying tears.

Each step forward, bold and bright,
Chasing shadows with new light.
With our hands, we break the chains,
In this power, love remains.

With the winds of change, we soar,
Finding hope in every door.
The sacred found in every end,
A new path where spirits blend.

In this journey, we arise,
Facing dawn with open eyes.
Every moment, blessed and true,
A sacred ground, for me and you.

Visions of Abundant Grace

In the stillness of the dawn,
He whispers hope anew,
With arms stretched wide in love,
He calls the weary through.

Each dawn unveils a promise,
A heart forever blessed,
With light that warms the humble,
And brings the soul to rest.

The rivers of His mercy flow,
An unceasing, gentle tide,
In every tear of sorrow,
His strength will be our guide.

In shadows deep, He walks with us,
Through valleys cloaked in night,
With visions of abundance,
He leads us to His light.

Through seasons of this journey,
We stand in faith's embrace,
Each moment, ever precious,
A gift of boundless grace.

Stories of the Redeemed

From ashes rise the faithful,
Each story a song of grace,
In the depths of brokenness,
They find their sacred place.

The wanderers return to Him,
With faith that's tried and true,
For every scar a testament,
To love that pulls us through.

With voices raised in unity,
We celebrate the lost,
In every heart transformed,
Their souls, our holy frost.

Each tale a thread of mercy,
Woven in the fabric grand,
A tapestry of faithfulness,
Crafted by His hand.

Through trials and through triumphs,
Together we proclaim,
The stories of the redeemed,
Forever praise His name.

The Prayer of Possibility

In the silence of our longing,
We lift our hearts in prayer,
For dreams that feel forgotten,
He meets us with His care.

With every whispered yearning,
The heavens bend to hear,
In faith's embrace, we ask Him,
And cast away all fear.

Hope flickers bright like starlight,
In the night of doubt we tread,
For with each breath of courage,
He speaks, and we are led.

In moments of despair,
When all seems far away,
The prayer of possibility,
Becomes our guiding ray.

So let our hearts be open,
To miracles He weaves,
In the tapestry of blessing,
Our spirits shall believe.

Embers of the Eternal

In the glow of evening's light,
Embers flicker through the night,
A warmth that holds a promise,
Of hope forever bright.

Each spark a whispered blessing,
From realms beyond our sight,
With every breath, a testament,
To grace that leads us right.

He breathes into the ashes,
Restoring what seems lost,
Through trials faced with courage,
New life emerges, glossed.

In the stillness of the moment,
His presence we embrace,
As embers glow with purpose,
In love, we find our place.

The dance of flames ignites,
A symphony divine,
In the embers of the eternal,
Our hearts forever shine.

Awakening of the Soul

In stillness, the heart begins to hear,
Whispers of truth that draw it near.
A light within begins to rise,
In humble prayer, the spirit flies.

Beneath the weight of silent night,
The soul awakens to sacred light.
With every breath, a new refrain,
Awakening calls, no longer in vain.

In radiant dawn, the shadows fade,
Each moment new, grace serenade.
From depths of doubt, a climb to grace,
A journey unfolds, a holy space.

With faith as wings, the heart takes flight,
In unity, we embrace the light.
Together we rise, hand in hand,
Awakening souls across the land.

Bound by love, in truth we stand,
An awakening shaped by divine hand.
In every heart, a beacon shines,
Guiding us home, where hope aligns.

The Dawn of Hope

As night retreats, the shadows wane,
A tender light breaks through the pain.
The dawn of hope shines ever bright,
Illuminating paths of right.

In whispered prayers, we find our way,
Through darkest nights to a glorious day.
With open hearts, we seek the grace,
Transforming fears to a warm embrace.

The sun ascends, the world awakes,
Each moment precious, a gift it makes.
From silent ashes, dreams arise,
In every tear, a new sunrise.

Together we stand, as one we strive,
In the dawn of hope, our spirits thrive.
With faith renewed, we journey forth,
In joy and love, we find our worth.

Let every soul sing of the light,
That glimmers bright, dispelling night.
For in this dawn, we're never alone,
In unity, together we're home.

From Ashes to Light

From ashes deep, a fire ignites,
Rebirth begins in the silent nights.
With every flicker, a promise made,
Out of the dark, our fears will fade.

Resilient hearts, we rise anew,
Embracing strength, a vision true.
In the warmth of love, we find our way,
From shadows cast, we seize the day.

The journey calls, both rough and bright,
From ashes scattered, we hold the light.
With hearts ablaze, we'll chart our course,
In every struggle, we find our source.

Through trials faced, our spirits soar,
From life's harsh winds, we learn to roar.
Together strong, our voices blend,
From ashes to light, our hearts ascend.

A testament of the soul's pure fight,
From depths of sorrow, we reach for height.
In every ember, hope's promise glows,
We rise as one, where true love flows.

The First Whisper of Grace

In silence deep, a voice does call,
A whisper soft as evening's fall.
The first light dawns within our soul,
In gentle grace, we feel made whole.

With every breath, the spirit sings,
Awakening joy, the heart takes wings.
In sacred moments, we find our pace,
The first whisper of unbounded grace.

Through trials faced, we gather strength,
In love's embrace, we travel length.
Each step a rhythm, divine and bright,
We are led forth into the light.

With open hearts, we roam the land,
In unity, together we stand.
The first whisper guides us through the night,
Like stars above, our dreams take flight.

In harmony, where all is tied,
The first whisper of grace, our joyful guide.
Together, we dance through joy and strife,
For love is the whisper that breathes us life.

Blessings in the Bloom

In the garden where dreams arise,
Gentle whispers kiss the skies.
Each petal holds a sacred grace,
A touch of Heaven in this place.

Sunlight dances on leaves so green,
A symphony of the unseen.
With every bloom, a prayer we weave,
In nature's arms, we learn to believe.

The fragrance lingers, pure and sweet,
A promise kept in every beat.
Through storms and trials, hope will soar,
Blessings abound forevermore.

Every season, a tale unfolds,
In the roots, a story told.
Bound by faith, we take our stand,
United in the Master's hand.

So let us cherish the gifts we gain,
With love's light, we rise from pain.
In this bloom, we find our way,
Guided by love, every day.

The Rise of Unbroken Spirits

In the stillness of the night,
Voices echo, spirits bright.
Through shadows deep, they find their song,
In every heart, where hope belongs.

With burdens heavy, souls unchained,
In faith's embrace, no fear remained.
The rise of spirits, fierce and bold,
United in love, their stories told.

Like phoenix flames that pierce the sky,
They lift their wings, prepared to fly.
From ashes of sorrow, strength is born,
In the dawn's light, no more forlorn.

Together they march, hand in hand,
Through valleys deep, a promised land.
With every step, a purpose clear,
Unbroken spirits persevere.

So let the echoes carry high,
A testament to the sky.
In every heart, their fire glows,
The rise of spirits, love bestows.

A Covenant of Change

In the circle of time and grace,
New beginnings take their place.
Each promise whispered, hearts align,
A covenant in sacred vine.

Through trials faced, we learn to grow,
With faith as our guide, we seek to know.
In every tear, a lesson learned,
For in the fire, our hearts are turned.

The seasons shift, yet love remains,
Through joy and sorrow, our hope sustains.
Together we journey, hand in hand,
In God's grand design, forever planned.

With every breath, we pledge anew,
To embrace the change that pulls us through.
In the tapestry woven, threads of light,
A promise to shine, to share the right.

So let the winds of change arise,
With open hearts, we reach the skies.
In unity, our spirits rise,
In this holy dance, we harmonize.

The Seraph's Call to Renewal

In the stillness, a voice prevails,
A seraph's call through winds and gales.
With wings of light, they soar and glide,
Inviting us to walk beside.

Through shadows cast, they gently sing,
Of love's embrace, eternal spring.
In the depths of silence, heed the call,
Awakening souls, uniting all.

In whispers soft, they speak of grace,
A journey beckons, time and space.
With every heartbeat, a chance to start,
To mend the seams of a broken heart.

As dawn breaks forth, hope fills the air,
In every spirit, a chance to care.
Together we rise, the call is clear,
In seraph's light, we leave our fear.

So let the melody guide our way,
In love's embrace, we find our stay.
Through renewal's path, we walk as one,
In the seraph's song, our journey's begun.

The Echo of Divine Songs

In the stillness, voices rise,
Whispers of love from the skies.
Harmony calls from realms above,
A melody wrapped in grace and love.

Hearts open wide to the sacred sound,
Each note a blessing, gently found.
In every echo, a truth ignites,
Guiding our souls through endless nights.

Let the rhythms of faith cascade,
In every moment, blessings made.
Resounding through valleys, soaring high,
The echo of divine songs, nigh.

Lift your hands to the heavens bright,
Feel the warmth of the spirit's light.
In unity, we sing and pray,
Together, we find our sacred way.

As the chorus swells, we rejoice,
In the grace, we find our voice.
With each heart, the song will grow,
In the echo, our spirits flow.

Inner Sanctum of Possibility

Within the heart, a garden blooms,
Softly whispering against our glooms.
Seeds of hope in the soil of grace,
A sanctum held in time and space.

In silence deep, creation flows,
From every breath, the spirit knows.
Limitless paths lie before our gaze,
In faith's embrace, we set ablaze.

Trust in the visions that softly ignite,
Guiding us through the darkest night.
Wisdom flows like a gentle stream,
We awaken to each vibrant dream.

Journey forth with courage to tread,
Through realms of doubt where angels led.
In the sanctum where echoes abide,
All things are possible, side by side.

With open hearts, we seek and find,
Truth that awakens the deepest mind.
In the inner sanctum, we will see,
The boundless gift of possibility.

A Chorus of Fresh Beginnings

Morning breaks with a radiant sigh,
Promises dance in the golden sky.
Each day unfolds like a blooming flower,
In every moment, we find our power.

Hope awakens with the sun's warm glow,
As the winds of change begin to flow.
Softly urging us to rise and sing,
A chorus blossoms in new offerings.

Let go of sorrows, embrace the light,
For every dawn brings renewed sight.
The universe speaks in colors bright,
In the chorus of life, we find our might.

With each breath, our spirits ignite,
Carving paths in the morning light.
In unison, we lift our voice,
In a symphony of love, we rejoice.

Together we weave this tapestry,
Of fresh beginnings and unity.
In harmony, our hearts will ring,
In the beauty of a new awakening.

Branches of Faithful Renewal

Roots grounded deep in sacred earth,
Branches reaching for divine rebirth.
In the stillness, whispers of truth,
Nurtured by the fountain of youth.

Seasons turn, and the leaves will fall,
Yet in stillness, we hear the call.
Faithful renewal in every breath,
Life is woven through love and death.

Embrace the storms that shape and mold,
Let every struggle turn to gold.
In the heart of winter, warmth we find,
Branches reaching as souls are entwined.

With every dawn, new life begins,
A testament of faith amidst our sins.
In the garden of souls, we bloom anew,
Together we rise, steadfast and true.

Through trials faced and lessons learned,
The light within us ever burned.
In branches of love, we find our grace,
Renewed in spirit, we embrace.

Incense of Fresh Beginnings

In the stillness, prayers rise,
Incense swirling towards the skies.
Each whisper carries hopes anew,
A fragrant promise, bright and true.

With dawn's light, burdens release,
Hearts awaken, finding peace.
The past is gone, let shadows fall,
In grace, we rise, together stand tall.

From ashes springs a vibrant soul,
Renewed by faith, we are made whole.
In every breath, the spirit sings,
Of boundless love and endless things.

Gathered round the sacred fire,
We kindle faith, our deep desire.
Each flicker tells of journeys vast,
With reverent hearts, we bless the past.

So let us walk this path divine,
With every step, His light will shine.
New beginnings in every prayer,
Together, we find grace to share.

Emerging Light of Hope

In darkest nights, a spark ignites,
A whisper calls, the heart alights.
Through trials faced, we stand in grace,
In hope's embrace, we find our place.

The morning dew, a sign divine,
With every drop, our spirits align.
Awakening dreams with gentle touch,
Each moment shared, it means so much.

With every breath, our faith we sow,
In fields of love, the seeds shall grow.
The path ahead may twist and turn,
But in our hearts, a fire will burn.

Rising sun, illuminate the way,
Guide us forth, come what may.
The promise of life, forever near,
In faith's strong tether, we cast out fear.

So let our voices fill the air,
In unity, we seek to share.
The light of hope will never cease,
With every step, we find our peace.

The Resurrection of Dreams

From silent graves, our dreams arise,
A gentle breath, beneath the skies.
With every hope, a chance restored,
In faith and love, our hearts are poured.

Awake, O soul, to life's embrace,
In every end, we find a trace.
Of visions lost, now set aglow,
With courage found, we let them flow.

The morning's call, a soft refrain,
With every drop, we wash our pain.
In stillness found, our spirits soar,
The resurrection, we can't ignore.

Past shadows fade, as love expands,
With open hearts, we join our hands.
In dreams reborn, we find our way,
Through faith's embrace, we greet the day.

So let us rise, in joy and grace,
To seek the light in every place.
With every heartbeat, hope redeems,
Together, we fulfill our dreams.

Kindling the Sacred Flame

In quiet chambers, the flame we light,
A sacred bond, we gather tight.
With hearts ablaze, our spirits rise,
To seek the truth that never lies.

The candles flicker, shadows dance,
In unity, we take our chance.
With whispered prayers, we hold the night,
Around this flame, our souls unite.

Each spark ignites a deeper call,
A love that shines beyond it all.
In moments shared, our burdens ease,
Together, we find solace and peace.

With hands extended, we share the glow,
In every heart, the truth will flow.
As sacred light draws near and near,
We kindle faith, dissolve our fear.

So let this flame forever blaze,
In every heart, let love raise.
Through trials faced and paths unknown,
In sacred light, we find our home.

The Light After the Storm

In the shadows, hope does rise,
Through thunderous trials, we find the skies.
Each raindrop whispers a sacred song,
Emerging strength, where we belong.

The winds may howl, yet hearts stay still,
In faith, we climb the highest hill.
For every tempest's fierce embrace,
Brings forth a glimpse of endless grace.

With every tear that dims the night,
The dawn unveils a softer light.
Embrace the path that's forged anew,
A world reborn, in colors true.

Through trials faced, our spirits soar,
In brokenness, we're made to explore.
Each lightning flash reveals the way,
To find the peace that bids us stay.

Thus, thank the storm that shaped the heart,
For in its wake, we're set apart.
The light that shines, a beacon bold,
A testament of love retold.

Brighter Paths in His Hands

In quiet moments, whispers flow,
Each step we take, He helps us grow.
Guided gently, our paths unwind,
In every heart, His love we find.

Through winding roads and hills so steep,
He cradles dreams, in trust we leap.
With every trial that seems to bind,
Release your fears, let grace remind.

In fields of hope, where faith runs free,
We glimpse the light, our destiny.
For every tear that marks the day,
Fosters resilience in its sway.

Across the valleys, His voice is clear,
In darkest hour, draw ever near.
A hand extended, with love profound,
In this embrace, our peace is found.

So take the step, don't shy away,
Brighter paths await, come what may.
In His embrace, the world expands,
With every heartbeat, His will stands.

The Divine Dance of Possibility

In the stillness, rhythms play,
A sacred tune that leads astray.
With open hearts, we learn to sway,
In divine dance, we find our way.

Each step a choice, each turn divine,
We glide in grace, as spirits intertwine.
In every struggle, joy ignites,
We are the stars, in endless nights.

With hands uplifted, we reach the sky,
Unveiling dreams that dare to fly.
In every heartbeat, a chance reborn,
To weave our hopes, no longer torn.

Through joyous leaps and gentle falls,
He beckons forth, our spirits call.
With reverence deep, we celebrate,
The wondrous path that love creates.

So let us dance, a vibrant song,
In unity, we all belong.
For in this circle, hand in hand,
We find our truth in His grand plan.

Yearning for the Sunrise

As night enfolds, our hearts awake,
A longing deep for dawn's sweet break.
In shadows cast, we seek the glow,
The warmth of faith, through every row.

Each moment still, as stars hold tight,
We gaze upon the distant light.
In prayers whispered, softly said,
A promise blooms, where hope is bred.

Through darkest hours, our spirits rise,
Longing fiercely for the skies.
For every dawn that brightly calls,
Reveals the grace that gently falls.

In each embrace of morning's kiss,
We taste the sweetness of His bliss.
With eyes alight, we greet the day,
In every heartbeat, grace will stay.

So yearn, dear soul, for skies so bright,
Where love transcends the depths of night.
In every sunrise, hearts prepare,
To dance in joy, in His tender care.

Renewal in the Spirit

In the stillness, hearts awake,
A whispering breeze, the soul to break.
With each dawn, hope's gentle light,
Guides the weary toward the right.

Roots reach deep in sacred earth,
From despair springs tender birth.
Grace flows down like a river wide,
Embracing all, a love untied.

In prayers soft, we find our peace,
With every breath, our fears release.
A dance of faith, a joyful song,
In unity, we all belong.

Let the spirit's fire ignite,
Transform our darkness into light.
Through storms we stand, our spirits soar,
Together bound, forevermore.

So rise, O hearts, in bright refrain,
Renewed in love, we cast out pain.
With open arms, the path is clear,
The spirit guides, we draw it near.

Rising from Ashes

From the charred remains, a spark ignites,
A phoenix born from darkest nights.
With every trial, the soul grows strong,
In the arms of grace, we all belong.

Hope's ember glows beneath the dust,
In the fire's warmth, we find our trust.
Through suffering's depths, we learn to see,
The light of love, our destiny.

In shadows cast by doubt and fear,
We rise anew, our vision clear.
With faith as our shield, we journey on,
To a brighter dawn, a new day drawn.

Each tear we've shed, a river flows,
Nurturing blooms where love bestows.
From the ashes, joy will bloom,
A testament to hope's sweet room.

Rejoice, dear hearts, in cycles true,
For every ending, life renews.
In unity, we take our flight,
And rise from ashes, pure and bright.

The Call of Unfolding

In the garden of the soul, we grow,
Petals soft amidst the snow.
Each bud a promise, every leaf,
A story woven, beyond belief.

The winds of change, they softly sing,
Inviting hearts to spread their wings.
Let go of fear, embrace the dawn,
In every ending, love is born.

As the sun's rays touch the earth,
Awakening all to new birth.
Answers hidden in silent grace,
A call to rise, our rightful place.

In stillness found, our spirits soar,
Together we seek a richer lore.
With open hearts, we shall not stray,
The path unfolds, come what may.

Trust the journey, follow the light,
In every shadow, find your insight.
Revel in this sacred dance,
The call of unfolding, a cosmic chance.

Whispers of the Divine

In quiet moments, hear the sighs,
Soft whispers from the endless skies.
Each heartbeat hums a sacred tune,
A melody beneath the moon.

In nature's breath, we find the call,
The sacred echoes, one and all.
Awake to love, let worries cease,
In every gaze, a soul's release.

The stars align in perfect grace,
An invitation to embrace.
Within our hearts, the light will shine,
A dance of spirit, truly divine.

Through trials faced, we learn to see,
The masterpiece of what can be.
With open arms, we greet the day,
And follow where the spirit sways.

So listen close to what's inside,
The whispers of the soul abide.
Embrace the path, both near and far,
For in the silence, love's the star.

A Bridge to Tomorrow

In faith we walk this sacred way,
With hearts alight, we rise and pray.
Each step a whisper, a song of grace,
Together we find our rightful place.

Through trials deep, we shall not stray,
For love endures, come what may.
The dawn will break, a shining clue,
A bridge to hope, a path anew.

With every breath, a chance to mend,
In unity, our spirits blend.
Through shadows cast, we seek the glow,
A bridge to tomorrow, where rivers flow.

In silence, we hear the ancient call,
To rise again, we cannot fall.
With open hearts, we dare to dream,
A bridge to futures, vast and supreme.

Embracing the Unseen

In quiet moments, truths unfold,
A tapestry of stories told.
With open hearts, we seek the light,
Embracing the unseen, taking flight.

Whispers of wisdom guide our way,
Through storm and calm, night and day.
In every breath, a sacred space,
We find the peace, the warm embrace.

Though shadows linger, hope shall rise,
With faith as wings, we'll touch the skies.
A journey deep, where spirits roam,
Embracing the unseen, we find our home.

Eternal love, a gentle stream,
In hearts ignited, we brightly beam.
Together as one, we walk this path,
In unity's glow, we escape wrath.

The Promise of Morning

With every dawn, a promise new,
The sun awakens, the skies turn blue.
In golden hues, we find our song,
The promise of morning, where we belong.

Each ray a reminder, grace abounds,
In every heartbeat, connection compounds.
Together we rise, our spirits soar,
The promise of morning, forevermore.

In stillness found, we breathe in trust,
A world of wonder, the sacred dust.
Hope blooms bright in the softest light,
The promise of morning, our guiding sight.

Through trials faced, we learn to see,
With open hearts, we can just be.
The dawn brings clarity, the night releases,
The promise of morning, as pain ceases.

Pathways to the Sacred

With every step, a path divine,
We seek the sacred, a love that shines.
In sacred spaces, we find our grace,
Pathways to the sacred, a warm embrace.

Through nature's whispers, the heart expands,
In unity's strength, we join our hands.
With open eyes, we see the signs,
Pathways to the sacred, where beauty aligns.

In every prayer, a soul is stirred,
In every moment, the heart is heard.
Together we journey through joy and pain,
Pathways to the sacred, forever remain.

As stars above show us the way,
In love's warm glow, we choose to stay.
In every heartbeat, truth reveals,
Pathways to the sacred, the spirit heals.

Forgiveness in the Air

In whispers soft, the heart will mend,
With love divine, we find our end.
Let go the chains that bind us tight,
In grace we rise, embracing light.

Each soul entwined, a sacred thread,
In mercy's arms, all pain is shed.
Forgive the past, let burdens cease,
In unity, we find our peace.

God's gentle hand, a guiding flame,
To those who walk in prayer's sweet name.
In every tear, the joy ascends,
For in forgiveness, love transcends.

No voice too small, no heart too broken,
Together we rise, a promise spoken.
With every breath, a chance to heal,
In harmony, our truths reveal.

Rejoice, O world, in kindness spread,
For forgiveness blooms where hate has fled.
In the act of grace, we find our share,
In every moment, forgiveness in the air.

A Psalm for Fresh Starts

In dawn's embrace, new hopes ignite,
With every sunrise, we take flight.
A heart renewed, washed by the rain,
In faith we trust, and lose our pain.

From shadows deep, we seek the way,
With open arms, we greet the day.
Each step we take, a sacred dance,
In life's great song, we find our chance.

Wounds may linger, but love transcends,
In every heart, a journey bends.
In humble prayer, we lift our voice,
For every soul, in Him rejoice.

With every breath, new mercies flow,
In trust we find the strength to grow.
Awakened spirits, rise and shine,
Embracing grace, a love divine.

A tapestry of dreams we weave,
In God's great plan, we all believe.
For fresh starts bloom, like flowers rare,
In every heart, His love laid bare.

The Seed of Revelation

In silent soil, a seed is sown,
The whispering truth, so deeply grown.
With faith as water, and hope the sun,
In shadows cast, our journey's begun.

Each tear a drop, a moment shared,
In love's embrace, we find we cared.
To seek the light, we raise our eyes,
With open hearts, we touch the skies.

The spark of wisdom, divine and pure,
In trials faced, our souls endure.
With open hands, release the doubt,
In every challenge, faith will sprout.

Let kindness bloom where anger stood,
In every act, our hearts do good.
The seed within, so rich and wild,
In every soul, God's love has smiled.

From darkness born, a bright new day,
The seed of truth will light the way.
In revelation, we rise and stand,
With every heartbeat, His guiding hand.

Transcendence Through Trials

In storms that rage, our spirits break,
Yet in the tempest, we shall awake.
With every wave, a lesson flows,
In trials faced, our courage grows.

What tempests shake can also mold,
A heart refined, a spirit bold.
Through darkest nights, the stars we chase,
In faith's embrace, we find our place.

With every fall, we rise anew,
In every tear, a vision true.
Through tests of fire, we carve our name,
In love's embrace, we fan the flame.

The path may twist, the road may bend,
But in each turn, His love transcends.
With eyes set high, and hearts aflame,
In each trial faced, we call His name.

For every trial that seeks to bind,
A spark of hope we always find.
Transcendence comes, a holy thrill,
Through darkest hours, we learn His will.

The Threshold of Tomorrow

At dawn's light, faith ignites,
With every heartbeat, hope ascends.
Paths unfold, shrouded in grace,
We step forth where love transcends.

Whispers of promise fill the air,
Guided by stars that brightly shine.
In the stillness, courage stands,
United in purpose, hearts align.

The journey unfolds, pure and true,
In every trial, we find our strength.
Together, we rise, hand in hand,
Through the shadows, we go the length.

With eyes set high, we seek the way,
In the quiet, His voice we hear.
Each moment a gift, a sacred chance,
To embrace tomorrow, free from fear.

The threshold beckons, let us cross,
In faith's embrace, we find our song.
Together as one, we forge ahead,
Where love abounds, we all belong.

Echoes of Redemption

In the silence, a whisper calls,
Echoes of grace in every heart.
Chains are broken where hope stands,
In shadows cast, we find the art.

Old burdens lifted, spirit free,
The past released, we see the light.
With open arms, He gathers us,
In every struggle, faith ignites.

Transformation blooms within the soul,
As we journey on this sacred quest.
In the mirror, we find our truth,
In His embrace, we find our rest.

Through valleys deep, and mountains high,
We walk the path, where mercy flows.
Forgiveness washes over pain,
In every step, new life bestows.

In united hearts, redemption sings,
A melody of love profound.
With every breath, we rise anew,
In echoes sweet, His grace is found.

The Holy Breath of Opportunity

Breathe in deep, the sacred air,
Each moment a chance to start anew.
In the hush, His spirit stirs,
Opening doors that lead to truth.

With grateful hearts, we seek the light,
Guiding us on this blessed path.
Every challenge, a lesson learned,
In His wisdom, we find our math.

Opportunities rise with the dawn,
Inviting us to step with grace.
Boldly we walk on faith's firm ground,
Finding joy in the sacred space.

The holy breath within us speaks,
With courage that dispels all doubt.
We take our steps in faithful trust,
In His embrace, we turn about.

As the sun sets on yesterdays,
New horizons come into view.
Embrace the journey that awaits,
In every heartbeat, His love is true.

A Pilgrimage of Peace

On this journey, we seek the calm,
With every step, the soul's delight.
Through valleys low and hills so high,
We follow stars that shine so bright.

In the quiet, wisdom whispers,
A gentle call to lift our gaze.
With hearts aligned, we march as one,
In peace's embrace, we find our ways.

With each encounter, we sow the seeds,
Of kindness, hope, and joy displayed.
In every heart, a sanctuary,
Where love resides and fears are laid.

Together we forge the path anew,
Hand in hand, through storms we'll tread.
In every trial, strength awakens,
Towards horizons where peace is spread.

The pilgrimage leads us closer still,
In unity, the world we mend.
Let love and grace be our guiding light,
As we journey on, until the end.

Circle of Restored Faith

In shadows deep, we find our way,
A flicker of light, the dawn of day.
Hearts once heavy, now lifted high,
With whispered prayers, we touch the sky.

In unity, we seek the truth,
Embracing love, recalling youth.
In every struggle, grace will flow,
Together stronger, hearts aglow.

Awake, arise, the spirit sings,
Through trials faced, new hope it brings.
With every step, our faith restores,
We tread as one, through open doors.

The circle turns, no end in sight,
In quiet moments, find the light.
Faith intertwined, our burdens shared,
In sacred bond, we are prepared.

Embrace each soul, a sacred trust,
In love united, pure and just.
The circle spins, a dance of grace,
In restored faith, we find our place.

The Sacred Cycle of Life

In the cradle of dawn, life takes flight,
From whispers of soil, to stars so bright.
Each heartbeat echoes, in sacred time,
A melody sung, a rhythm sublime.

The seasons turn, a divine embrace,
In growth and decay, we find our place.
From joy to sorrow, we gently flow,
Life's tapestry woven, thread by thread we sow.

Through storms and calm, we journey far,
Guided by faith, beneath the stars.
In every challenge, resilience stands,
The sacred cycle, in loving hands.

With every sunrise, hope is reborn,
In tears we cherish, in laughter, adorn.
Connections woven, with love's design,
In life's sacred dance, our spirits align.

Let us honor this path we tread,
From cradle to grave, with love we're fed.
In unity, we rise and strive,
In the sacred cycle, we truly thrive.

Veils of New Horizons

When morning breaks with softest glow,
The veils of doubt begin to go.
With open hearts and spirits wide,
We welcome change, and stretch with pride.

A tapestry of colors bright,
Unfolds before our seeking sight.
In every shadow, light will chase,
New horizons, a warm embrace.

With faith as guide, we stand as one,
Embracing what has just begun.
Through trials faced, we'll rise anew,
In every moment, grace breaks through.

Veils lifted high, our burdens cease,
In love, we find a deeper peace.
With open hands and lifted eyes,
We journey forth, where wisdom lies.

The path ahead, though unclear still,
With every step, we bend our will.
In veils of new horizons, we rise,
With faith entwined, we touch the skies.

The Covenant of Hope

In whispered vows beneath the stars,
We find our peace amidst the scars.
With every breath, the promise renews,
The covenant born where love ensues.

Through trials faced and sorrows deep,
In every moment, our faith we keep.
A light in darkness, a guiding hand,
In the covenant of hope, together we stand.

With hearts ablaze, we rise as one,
In every battle, victory won.
Through stormy nights, we hold the flame,
In the covenant of hope, we're not the same.

Let every soul feel love's embrace,
In unity, we find our place.
Through kindness shown, we heal the past,
In the sacred bond, our love will last.

The journey calls with open arms,
Drawing us close, with gentle charms.
In the covenant of hope we sing,
A melody of grace, our hearts take wing.

Awakening Dawn

In the stillness of morn, we rise,
Heaven's whispers fill the skies.
With each breath, a chance to see,
The light that sets our spirits free.

Golden rays break the night,
Guiding hearts toward what is right.
In peace, we find our sacred song,
As we journey where we belong.

The world adorned in colors bright,
Nature blooms in pure delight.
In each petal, a prayer unfolds,
A promise of hope, forever told.

We lift our voices in praise and song,
To the Creator, to whom we belong.
For each dawn is a chance to renew,
In faith and love, we start anew.

So let the sun warm our soul,
As we embrace the divine goal.
Awake, arise, and take your stand,
In the embrace of God's gentle hand.

Graceful Resurgence

In the shadows, faith may wane,
Yet love's embrace will remain.
With every fall, we rise again,
In His mercy, we're freed from pain.

Life's tempest may shake the ground,
But in silence, solace is found.
Hope rekindles the weary heart,
In the dance of dreams, we won't part.

With each trial, our spirits soar,
To the heavens, we seek and implore.
In time's embrace, we find our way,
Guided by light through the fray.

Grace flows like rivers, unconfined,
Awakening dreams once left behind.
In this moment, we claim our place,
In the arms of eternal grace.

Together, we weave a tapestry,
Threads of faith, love, and unity.
In every heartbeat, we discern,
That through grace, we shall return.

The First Light of Faith

When darkness casts a heavy shroud,
A flicker of faith stands tall and proud.
In the quiet, a promise is made,
That hope does flourish, never to fade.

The first light touches weary minds,
With warmth and clarity, it binds.
In each moment, truth unfolds,
A sanctuary where love enfolds.

In the realm where doubts reside,
The first light shines, our steadfast guide.
Through valleys low, we walk in trust,
With every step, in God we must.

As morning breaks, our hearts ignite,
With every prayer, we reignite.
The first light glimmers, a sacred vow,
To live in faith, here and now.

So let us journey, hand in hand,
Through the wonders of this promised land.
In the first light of faith, we find,
A spirit uplifted, a soul aligned.

In the Garden of Hope

In the garden where dreams renew,
Petals bloom and skies are blue.
Each blossom sings a sacred tune,
Beneath the watchful, loving moon.

Here, our troubles cease to be,
In stillness, we find serenity.
With every seed that we shall sow,
In faith, we nurture love to grow.

The fragrance of grace fills the air,
In this haven, we find our care.
Beneath God's gaze, our spirits soar,
In the garden, we are restored.

Through trials faced, we find our chance,
In every tear, the soul's advance.
Within this space of gentle light,
Hope reborn in the darkest night.

So let us wander, hearts aflame,
In the garden, we praise His name.
For in hope's embrace, we thrive,
Together, in love, we come alive.

The Journey Beyond Yesterday

In shadows cast by time's great hand,
We wander forth, where dreams expand.
With faith our guide, through trials we tread,
Towards the dawn, where hope is spread.

Each step we take, a whispered prayer,
A melody of love in the air.
Beyond the past, our spirits soar,
To realms of peace, forevermore.

With hearts alight on paths of grace,
We seek the truth, we seek His face.
For every heartache leads us near,
To promises bright, dispelling fear.

The road is long, yet we embrace,
The joy of faith, the sweet embrace.
With open hearts, we share the light,
As stars shine forth, in darkest night.

And in the end, when we arrive,
In love's pure glow, our souls revive.
With yesterday behind us, strong,
In unity, we journey on.

Blossoms in Divine Tending

In gardens where the spirits play,
The blossoms dance, in bright array.
Each petal soft, a tale unfolds,
Of grace unbound, and love retold.

With tender hands, the Lord does sow,
The seeds of joy, where rivers flow.
In every bloom, a sign divine,
A testament of love's design.

Through storms we face, through darkest nights,
His gentle touch brings forth the light.
With every breath, the sacred sings,
Of hope renewed, and brighter things.

We are the flowers in His care,
Each moment shared, a precious prayer.
Together we rise, with courage bold,
In sun's embrace, our hearts unfold.

To nourish souls, to lift the weak,
In every word, His love we speak.
Blossoms of faith, in harmony,
We flourish in His majesty.

The Sacred Embrace of Tomorrow

With arms outstretched to greet the dawn,
We find the strength to carry on.
Each breath a gift, in grace we'll stand,
Together bound, hand in hand.

In every moment, wisdom flows,
A sacred truth that gently grows.
To face the trials, we are bold,
In love entwined, a tale unfolds.

The future calls with whispers sweet,
A melody where hearts will meet.
With faith as lantern, brightly shone,
We pave the path, lest we roam alone.

Embracing change, we open wide,
The door to hope, our faithful guide.
The sacred trust that lies ahead,
A promise kept, where angels tread.

With every sunrise, light we see,
In unity, we shall be free.
Tomorrow waits with open arms,
A tapestry of endless charms.

Wandering into the Light

Through valleys deep, where shadows creep,
We wander forth, our faith to keep.
With lanterns bright, we find our way,
In search of love, we yearn and pray.

Each gentle breeze, a whisper soft,
Reminds us of the call aloft.
In every heart, the spark ignites,
A journey blessed, towards the lights.

We lift our eyes to skies anew,
With every step, our spirits grew.
In trust we walk, through trials faced,
A path of hope, divinely graced.

The dawn will break, the night will cease,
In sacred peace, our souls release.
With open hearts, we embrace the call,
To rise as one, transcending all.

And as we wander, hand in hand,
In unity, we make our stand.
For in the light, we'll find our place,
A lasting home, a warm embrace.

Divine Threads of Tomorrow

In whispers soft, the heavens weave,
A tapestry where dreams believe.
With every thread, a promise spun,
A guiding light, a new day's sun.

The stars align with gentle grace,
As faith ignites each sacred space.
In paths unseen, the Spirit flows,
In every heart, a seedling grows.

With open arms, we face the dawn,
Each challenge met, together drawn.
In unity, our purpose glows,
As love's embrace forever shows.

Through trials faced, we find our way,
In prayers whispered, night and day.
With courage forged in holy fire,
We rise anew, our souls aspire.

Through darkest nights, and stormy seas,
The guiding hand brings us to peace.
With hearts entwined, we journey on,
In every step, God's will be strong.

Hearts in Bloom

In gardens wild, where spirits play,
Hearts open wide to greet the day.
With petals soft and colors bright,
They sing of love's purest light.

Each raindrop falls, a soft caress,
Nurturing hope, divine finesse.
In every bud, a tale revealed,
A promise made, a truth concealed.

As sunbeams dance on tender leaves,
Awakening all that nature weaves.
With gentle hands, we tend the ground,
In joy and grace, our souls are found.

Together strong, we rise as one,
In sacred bonds, our race begun.
With love's embrace and hearts in tune,
We blossom forth, like flowers in June.

Through seasons change, our roots run deep,
In faith we trust, in dreams we leap.
With every heart, a story sown,
In unity, we've truly grown.

The Alchemy of Change

In twilight's grasp, the old gives way,
To whispered truths that guide our sway.
With every ending, new begins,
In cycles spun, the soul transcends.

The chalice filled with lessons learned,
In alchemy, our spirits burned.
With fragile hands, we shape our fate,
Transforming fear into love's state.

Each trial faced, a golden key,
Unlocking doors to what will be.
With joy we dance in shadows cast,
Embracing change, we grow steadfast.

With faith as fuel, we rise anew,
In every heart, the Spirit's view.
Through storms and calm, our spirits soar,
In love's embrace, forevermore.

In unity, we sing our song,
A symphony where all belong.
With every breath, we write the page,
In this divine alchemy of change.

Holy Horizons Ahead

Beyond the tears, the light does break,
A promise held for all our sake.
In holy whispers, hope does rise,
Awakening dreams beneath the skies.

The dawn unfolds, a sacred hue,
Each heart ignites, a path anew.
With faith as guide, we journey forth,
To greet the joy, to seek the worth.

With open eyes, we see the grace,
In every step, in every space.
As souls align upon this quest,
To share the love, to seek the best.

Through valleys low and mountains high,
We lift our hearts, we soar and fly.
In holy trust, we rise like doves,
A testament to faith and love.

The horizon calls, a beacon bright,
With courage strong, we chase the light.
In every heart, the Spirit's thread,
Unites us all, our paths are led.

The Journey Towards Light's Embrace

In shadows deep, we wander lost,
Seeking truth, no matter the cost.
With hope as our guide, we step with grace,
Towards the warm glow of love's embrace.

Through trials faced, our spirits soar,
Yearning for peace, forevermore.
Each footfall echoes a sacred song,
A melody where hearts belong.

The path is long, but light draws near,
Washing away the doubt and fear.
In unity, we rise and stand,
Together as one, hand in hand.

With faith, we lift our eyes so bright,
Embracing the dawn, dispelling the night.
In every moment, grace we find,
The journey unfolding, our hearts aligned.

Let love's embrace be our guiding star,
Shining brightly, no matter how far.
In the sacred light, our souls will meet,
The journey to joy becomes complete.

Sacred Resurgence in the Shadows

In silence deep, where whispers dwell,
The spirit stirs, breaking the shell.
From ashes rise, the soul restored,
In shadows felt, the heart is poured.

With every tear, a lesson learned,
In darkness, flickers of light discerned.
The sacred path, though rugged and steep,
Bears fruits of peace that gently seep.

Awake, arise, the dawn is near,
In every struggle, cast away fear.
With courage clenched, we take a stand,
Embracing hope, each heart a brand.

The cycle turns, rebirth unfolds,
In sacred whispers, our truth is told.
Let love ignite the flame anew,
In shadows' dance, our spirits grew.

Together we mend, together we rise,
Finding solace in the skies.
For in each shadow, light will gleam,
An everlasting, radiant dream.

Inspiring the Divine Within

Within our hearts, the light does dwell,
A spark of love, a sacred well.
With every breath, we connect and weave,
The divine presence, we believe.

In stillness found, the ego fades,
A inner peace that never trades.
With open eyes, we start to see,
The beauty found in simply being free.

The whispers soft, they guide our way,
Creating paths where souls can sway.
In trust, we step, our spirits raised,
Inspiring light, in praise we're blazed.

With gentle hands, we share this gift,
Providing love, giving hearts a lift.
Together we shine, as one we sing,
In unity's dance, our spirits take wing.

Let every thought, each word be kind,
Awakening love that's intertwined.
For in this life, our souls proclaim,
The divine essence, forever the same.

The Mandate of Now

The present moment, a sacred call,
In breaths we take, we find it all.
With stillness pure, the world we face,
The mandate of now, a holy space.

In every heartbeat, a chance to be,
To live with purpose, wild and free.
Let go of burdens, release the weight,
In this moment, let love create.

Embrace the now, for time stands still,
A gift to cherish, to shape our will.
With open hands, the future unfolds,
In vibrant hues, our story told.

The whispers of fate beckon us near,
In faith and trust, we conquer fear.
Be present, dear heart, in this dance of time,
For now is sacred, a holy rhyme.

In every instant, divine light gleams,
Filling our lives with radiant dreams.
Together we rise, here and now,
The mandate of love, let us avow.

The Spirit's Invitation to Change

Awaken your heart, let love lead the way,
Embrace the whispers, welcome the new day.
In shadows of doubt, find the courage to rise,
For change is a blessing in the Spirit's wise eyes.

Each moment a chance, each breath a new song,
Transformation calls, inviting us along.
Let go of the past, hold tightly to grace,
In the dance of renewal, discover your place.

The Spirit invites, with arms open wide,
In joy and in sorrow, the journey's our guide.
With faith as our cloak, we gently embrace,
The sacred unfolding of our life's pace.

In the garden of growth, tend seeds of your soul,
From ashes to beauty, let love make you whole.
With each step of faith, let courage ignite,
The path of transformation shines ever so bright.

So heed the call's echo, let the heart sway,
For change is the Spirit, lighting our way.
With unity and hope, and a heart that's aflame,
We rise to the challenge, in the Spirit's name.

The Radiance of Beginnings

In dawn's gentle light, new journeys unfold,
A canvas of dreams, painted bright and bold.
Each sunrise a promise, a whisper of bliss,
In the heart of the faithful, the radiance exists.

Awakening souls, with visions afresh,
In the sacred embrace, we find our true flesh.
The whispers of morning, soft glimmers of grace,
Invite us to dance in the source we embrace.

The compass of faith leads us nearer to truth,
To cherish the wisdom that flows from our youth.
With open hearts, we rise to the thrill,
Of beginnings uncharted, our spirits to fill.

Each moment a gift, wrapped in love's warm light,
For every new path holds stars shining bright.
With gratitude spoken, let our spirits sing,
For in the embrace of the dawn, we take wing.

So breathe in the morning, let hope be your song,
In the radiance of beginnings, we all belong.
With faith as our anchor, we welcome the sea,
In each cherished moment, we live truly free.

Rewriting Our Sacred Stories

In the tapestry woven of timeless lore,
We hold sacred tales, so rich at the core.
With ink of the heart and a pen made of light,
We gather our courage, ready to write.

Each chapter a blessing, a lesson refined,
With spaces for healing, the Spirit aligned.
From chains of the past, to new wings of flight,
We rewrite our stories, igniting the night.

In whispers of truth, we find our own voice,
Transcending the shadows, we make a new choice.
With love as our guide, and compassion our shield,
The canvas of life, with grace, is revealed.

So gather the fragments of courage within,
With the brush of forgiveness, let healing begin.
In the space of reflection, our spirits take form,
Together we shine through each challenge and storm.

Rewriting our stories, let the heart steer,
For in each revelation, the path becomes clear.
Embracing the journey, let the soul sing,
With love in our hearts, we embrace everything.

The Tapestry of Tomorrow's Dreams

In the loom of our hopes, threads of light intertwine,
We weave a tomorrow, rich and divine.
With visions aflame, and aspirations aglow,
We forge a bright destiny, together we sow.

In the silence of night, sweet whispers unfold,
Promising tales that are yet to be told.
So gather your dreams, let them dance in the air,
For in the heart's fabric, we find solace there.

Each stitch of intention creates a new path,
While love's gentle hand holds back the world's wrath.
With faith as our compass, we journey ahead,
In the tapestry woven, the Spirit is spread.

In unity we stand, as the stars do align,
To paint the horizons, a vision divine.
With vibrant connections, let kindness be seen,
As we craft the tomorrow of our sacred dream.

So nurture the threads that connect us in grace,
For together we'll shine in this mystical space.
In the tapestry's glow, where we all belong,
Let love guide the way, and our hearts make a song.

Cascades of Abundant Grace

From heaven's heights, blessings pour,
Gentle whispers forevermore.
In every heart, hope ignites,
A symphony of shining lights.

Streams of mercy, flowing free,
In silent prayer, we find the key.
Beneath the stars, our spirits soar,
Wrapped in love, forevermore.

Radiant dawn, a sacred gift,
In humble grace, our souls uplift.
Each step we take, His path we tread,
With faith as guide, we shall be led.

Mountains rise, yet faith stands tall,
His gentle voice, it calls us all.
Through trials faced, we find our way,
In His embrace, we bend and sway.

In every moment, His presence near,
A steady hand to calm our fear.
With every breath, our praise we raise,
In cascades of abundant grace.

Journey Through the Wilderness

In shadows deep, we wander lost,
Yet in our hearts, we trust the cost.
Through barren lands, our spirits cry,
Yet whispers soft from God on high.

With every step, the path unclear,
We find our strength in faithful cheer.
The desert tests both will and soul,
Yet in His love, we are made whole.

Clouds of doubt, they swirl around,
But faith will anchor, firmly bound.
Through trials fierce, we seek His face,
A journey carved in endless grace.

Every tear, a seed of hope,
In silence deep, we learn to cope.
Through rugged paths, His light will shine,
In wilderness, the heart aligns.

For every scar, a story told,
In God's embrace, we find the bold.
With open hearts, we walk and pray,
Through wilderness, we find our way.

Rebirth in Light's Embrace

In twilight's glow, the dawn will rise,
From ashes lost, new life will sigh.
With every breath, resurrection calls,
In radiant light, our spirit thralls.

The night retreats, and shadows fade,
In love's embrace, our fears are laid.
With open arms, we welcome grace,
In every heart, a sacred place.

Each moment breathes a chance to grow,
Through trials faced, our faith will show.
In petals soft, rebirth we find,
Through light's embrace, we leave behind.

In quiet realms, the soul will soar,
With every prayer, we seek much more.
Through darkest nights, His promise stands,
In light's embrace, we heal our lands.

And as we rise, like phoenix flight,
In every heart, His love ignites.
For in His grace, we find the way,
In rebirth's glow, we seek the day.

The Lament of Yesterday

Beneath the weight of shattered dreams,
In silent nights, the sorrow schemes.
With whispered prayers, we seek to mend,
The pieces broken, hearts to tend.

Reflections haunt, shadows entwine,
In past's embrace, we search for signs.
Yet every tear, a lesson learned,
Through trials faced, our hearts have turned.

In every ache, remembrance sings,
Of love once lost and fleeting things.
But from the depths, a promise springs,
In time's embrace, a new song rings.

The lessons carved in scars we bear,
With every sorrow, burdens share.
For in lament, a truth we find,
That light brings hope, and we unwind.

So let us rise from shadows past,
In gratitude, our spirits cast.
For every moment, pain will fade,
In love's embrace, our souls are made.

Song of the Unfolding

In whispers soft, the dawn awakes,
With golden light and gentle grace.
Nature sings a hymn of hope,
As hearts arise, and spirits elope.

Each petal blooms with sacred breath,
A dance of life, defying death.
In every leaf, a story told,
Of faith reborn, in love upheld.

The heavens echo blessings near,
With every prayer, we draw them near.
In unity, we stand as one,
In gratitude, our souls are spun.

Through trials faced, we find our way,
Guided by light, come what may.
With every step, we seek the kind,
A deeper truth, within aligned.

So let us sing, with hearts ablaze,
In the unfolding of our days.
For in the light, we learn to see,
The sacred threads that weave the free.

In the Garden of Today

Upon the soil, our dreams take root,
In every heart, a tender shoot.
Love's gentle hand, it tends with care,
In this garden, divinity's share.

The sun will rise, the rain will fall,
Each moment speaks, a sacred call.
With open arms, we greet the day,
In unity, we find our way.

Amongst the blooms, we lift our song,
In harmony, where we belong.
The fragrance sweet, of hope divine,
In every glance, Your light we find.

Through seasons change, the Spirit moves,
In quiet whispers, love improves.
With faith like seeds, we plant our dreams,
And watch them flourish, as love redeems.

In gratitude for life's embrace,
We walk together, filled with grace.
This garden blooms with joy and peace,
In every moment, sweet release.

The Covenant of Each New Dawn

With morning light, new promises wake,
The earth exhales for hope's own sake.
In every breath, renew our vow,
To cherish life, in the here and now.

The skies unfold, a tapestry bright,
Each star a whisper of love's delight.
In faith we stand, hand in hand,
With gentle hearts, we understand.

For trials faced, they shape our path,
In sacred love, we find our math.
Through shadows deep, we learn to shine,
In every soul, the divine design.

As dawn arises, let spirits soar,
With every heartbeat, crave for more.
In unity, we find our grace,
In every challenge, love's embrace.

The covenant made, we shall uphold,
In every moment, truth be told.
With gratitude, our hearts align,
In the rhythm of the divine.

Promises in the Soil

From humble earth, the blessings grow,
In every seed, a promise showed.
With faith we sow, our hopes take flight,
In the darkest hours, we seek the light.

The roots run deep, a sacred bond,
In every heart, a quiet pond.
With patience, we wait, for love to rise,
In every trial, the Spirit flies.

As sunlight breaks, the shadows fade,
In trust, we find the path we've made.
With open hands, we share our gain,
In every loss, the love remains.

The harvest comes, a gift so pure,
In unity, we feel secure.
With gratitude for all we've sown,
In the soil of faith, we have grown.

So let us nurture this sacred place,
With love and kindness, fill our space.
In promises kept, we find our way,
In every heartbeat, a new today.

Shadows Giving Way to Grace

In the hush of the night, hope shines bright,
Breaking the spell of a long, weary plight.
With a whisper of faith, our doubts take flight,
Embracing the dawn, where darkness meets light.

Every tear that has fallen, a price we pay,
For the love that awaits, come what may.
In the valley of shadows, we learn to pray,
Finding strength in our hearts, as we seek His way.

The past may hold chains, but grace sets us free,
In the warmth of His love, we dance by the sea.
With every step forward, we choose to believe,
That shadows can vanish, like mist on the lea.

Faith is the anchor that holds through the storm,
Turning ashes to beauty, we vow to transform.
In the light of His presence, our spirits warm,
Shadows giving way, His love will adorn.

So let us walk boldly, hand in hand with grace,
With hope as our compass, we run life's race.
In the arms of the Savior, we find our place,
Emerging from shadows, our spirits embrace.

The Eternal Cycle of Faith

In the depths of despair, faith finds a way,
A flicker of hope at the break of day.
Through trials we journey, come what may,
Knowing grace surrounds us, ever to stay.

Each promise spoken, like seeds in the ground,
In the garden of hearts, His love can be found.
With patience we nurture, our souls profound,
The cycle of faith, where blessings abound.

When burdens grow heavy, and paths seem unclear,
We rise on the wings of unyielding prayer.
Through valleys and mountains, the Savior draws near,
In the eternal dance, we surrender our fear.

Light pierces darkness, revealing the true,
In the heartbeat of grace, we know what to do.
With every season, He comforts anew,
The eternal cycle, our spirits imbue.

Trust in the journey, let each moment sing,
For faith is a treasure, an everlasting spring.
In unity and love, all souls take wing,
The cycle of faith, in His name we cling.

Stars Born from Darkness

In the silence of night, stars begin to gleam,
Born from the shadows, where dreams weave a seam.
Each light a reminder, of hope's radiant beam,
Emerging from darkness, they shimmer and teem.

Through trials we stumble, our spirits may bend,
But in the abyss, we find strength to mend.
With every small flicker, faith becomes our friend,
Guiding us forward, on love we depend.

For every lost soul, there's a light to restore,
A promise of peace, when we seek and implore.
In the vastness of night, we find something more,
Stars born from darkness, forever we soar.

Through time's gentle hand, we learn to embrace,
The beauty in struggle, the path that we trace.
In the tapestry woven, our scars leave their grace,
Stars shining brightly, in our rightful place.

So let us remember, when shadows arise,
The promise of light, that pierces the skies.
In the heart of the night, a new dawn never lies,
Stars born from darkness, our spirits will rise.

Flights of the Faithful Heart

With wings of devotion, we lift our gaze,
Breaking the chains of life's fleeting maze.
In the warmth of His love, we find our ways,
Soaring through heavens, in a glorious blaze.

Each burden a feather, lightening the load,
Guided by grace, on this sacred road.
With trust in His promise, our hearts are bestowed,
Flights of the faithful, a gift we uphold.

When storms fill the skies, our spirits ignite,
Like eagles in flight, embracing the height.
With courage our compass, we embrace the night,
In the glow of His presence, everything feels right.

With every dawn breaking, new journeys we start,
Reviving our spirits, igniting the heart.
Through trials and triumphs, we play our part,
In the symphony woven, of faith's sacred art.

So let us believe, and forever depart,
On flights of the faithful, with joy, we impart.
In the arms of the Savior, our lives we chart,
Faithful hearts soaring, love's incredible start.

A Breath of the Ancients

In whispered hymns of sacred lore,
The echoes of time softly implore.
With each stepping stone, as faith does tread,
The wisdom of ages gently spread.

Through twilight's veil, the past does glow,
Guiding the seeker where rivers flow.
In stillness found, the heart will sing,
Embracing the truth that dawn will bring.

With hands uplifted to stars above,
We find the path, a thread of love.
In the quiet, ancient realms align,
We breathe the spirit, eternally divine.

The mountains stand, a steadfast wall,
Guardians whisper, hear their call.
Through valleys deep and shadows cast,
We carry the light, a flame steadfast.

As night departs, the morn awakes,
In sacred ground, the spirit shakes.
With prayerful hearts and voices entwined,
We walk the journey our souls designed.

Invocations of New Dawn

Awake, arise, the sun breaks free,
Its golden rays, a clarion plea.
To cleanse the shadows, heal the night,
With every heartbeat, embrace the light.

The world stirs softly with hope anew,
In every drop of morning dew.
With lifted hands, we gather grace,
As love unites in this sacred place.

Through prayers woven in the air,
We sing of peace, a vision rare.
Embrace the whispers, the stories told,
The bond of ages, forever bold.

Let unity rise, a chorus strong,
In harmony's embrace, where we belong.
With faith like rivers, it flows profound,
In every heartbeat, the truth is found.

In the dawn's embrace, a promise lies,
A world transformed beneath the skies.
Through sacred ritual, our voices blend,
Invoking blessings, love without end.

Seeking the Celestial

In starlit nights, our dreams take flight,
Guided by beams of ethereal light.
We wander forth, with hope as our shield,
In the vastness, the heart is revealed.

The cosmos whispers, secrets unfold,
In the tapestry of life, we're bold.
With eyes like galaxies, we yearn to see,
The patterns of destiny, wild and free.

Through vibrant fields where starlight dances,
Each heartbeat a chance, each moment advances.
In sacred spaces, divinity calls,
We rise together, as darkness falls.

With souls entwined, a luminous thread,
We chase the visions where angels tread.
In communion with all, we delve deep,
Awake in the journey, we dare to leap.

As we seek the celestial, hand in hand,
In the realm of dreams, we understand.
With faith as our compass, we're never alone,
In the universe's heart, we find our home.

Refuge of the Resilient

In storms that brew and tempests roar,
The resilient heart finds strength to soar.
Through trials faced, we gather round,
In the refuge where hope is found.

Life's light may flicker, yet never cease,
For in the struggle, we discover peace.
With spirits forged in fire and grace,
We rise together, our sacred space.

In the embrace of earth, strong and true,
We cultivate love, like morning dew.
With open arms, we share our plight,
In the refuge of community's light.

With echoes of prayers, we carry on,
In unity's strength, the fear is gone.
The resilient soul, like a sturdy tree,
Bears witness to trials, yet wild and free.

Through shadows long, we seek the dawn,
In the strength of many, we press on.
With hearts like rivers, flowing sincere,
The refuge of the resilient draws near.

Milton Keynes UK
Ingram Content Group UK Ltd.
UKHW020040271124
451585UK00012B/966

9 789916 79201